T0114968

Echoes Of A Whisper

Lughano Mwangwegho

Langaa Research & Publishing CIG
Mankon, Bamenda

Publisher:
Langaa RPCIG
Langaa Research & Publishing Common Initiative Group
P.O. Box 902 Mankon
Bamenda
North West Region
Cameroon
Langaagrp@gmail.com
www.langaa-rpcig.net

Distributed in and outside N. America by African Books Collective
orders@africanbookscollective.com
www.africanbookscollective.com

ISBN-10: 9956-764-07-8

ISBN-13: 978-9956-764-07-5

© Lughano Mwangwegho 2017

DISCLAIMER
All views expressed in this publication are those of the author and do not
necessarily reflect the views of Langaa RPCIG.

Dedication

In memory of my late mother, Ellen
Who lost her battle to cancer and died on 2nd August
2014 – RIP

Table of Contents

Acknowledgements..ix

Part One: *From Within and Without*................1

A Redemption Song...3
When a Woman is Fed UP.. 4
A Web of Injustice...5
A Snake in the Forest...6
The Other Woman..7
Let's Talk About Love.. 8
Promise Me My Love... 9
A Love Poem..10
A Man in the House is Worth Two
in the Street...11
An Encounter with a Mother-in-l.a.w.......................12
Lessons worth Learning...13
The Dream.. 14
You Lied.. 15
Nobody's Own... 16
On the Wedding Day... 17
Behind a Man's Downfall.. 18
Crying Over Spilt Milk... 19
A Virtuous Woman.. 20
A False Lover... 22
Who Must Reap the Harvest?.................................... 23
Black Pride.. 24
The Tale of a Chicken..25
A Woman's Secret.. 26

The Journey..27

Fruits of his Labor...29

Dust in the Calabash...30

I am not a Child... 31

When the Sun Rises.. 32

A Foreigner in One's Land.................................. 33

The Choice of the Heart.......................................34

The Woman Next Door...35

The Train.. 36

A Word to My Son...37

You will not Eat of this Tree............................... 38

A Letcher in the Yard... 39

How?... 40

She is the Roots.. 41

A Well by the Roadside...42

Part Two: *Messages from no where*..................**43**

Old Sweet Days... 45

In these Times.. 46

The Lazybones..47

A Funeral of a Mad Man...................................... 48

The Voices...49

The Village Spectacle... 50

My Mother...51

Fold Your Legs Grandpa...................................... 52

Sundown at Mwenilondo...................................... 53

Samples of Fortune.. 55

Where is God? 56

The Departure...57

I Will Rest when I am Dead..................................58

Kwazulu-Natal Revisited......................................59

Will you be There? 60
A Living Myth.. 61
In Dilemma... 62
The Dance.. 63
Waiting with Hope... 64
Of Pastors and Offerings................................. 65
Do not Laugh.. 66
Uhuru Mother, Uhuru...................................... 67
Memoires of an Immigrant................................. 68
Elegy to the Slave Master................................ 69
Testimonies... 70
On Rwandan Genocide....................................... 71
Black Child, Son of Earth................................ 73
At the Crossroads.. 74
Cries in the Torrents.................................... 75
Silence... 76
Only My Mother.. 77
The Warmonger... 78
The Last Walk... 79
Dust in the Whirlwind.................................... 80
Like Father, Like Son.................................... 81
Echoes of a Whisper...................................... 82

Acknowledgements

I wish to extend my gratitude to the following media organizations for their unprecedented support by relentlessly according my short-stories and poems space in their editions: Malawi News, the Sunday Times, Saturday Nation and Moni Magazine.

The list would be incomplete if I didn't mention the following people whose moral support and encouragement contributed to the writing of this book: James Chavula, Temwani Mgunda, McNeil Timothy Kalowekamo whose love for poetry is immense and is ready to read anything written in stanzas; Willy Jones Mwangwegho jnr who read and analysed most of the poems before publication, and in some cases he gave opinion on some; Otteria Bwighane Kayuni, a teacher at Chivala primary school whose inspirational talk gave birth to a number of poems in this collection, lastly but not least, Joanna Woods whose name must always be mentioned when poetry is the subject.

Part One

From Within and Without

A Redemption Song

I am no longer a woman of the kitchen
Whose eyes are red with smoke
I am not the woman whose buttocks
You whip with a chain
And nose poke with a fork
When you are drunk

I am no longer a sex slave
The woman who quenches your lust
And whose womb you scorch with desire
I am not the woman you sleep with in a cave
And spoil her hair with dust
When she refuses to open her legs

I am no longer the woman of the forest
Whose day ends gathering fire-wood
For brewing beer or baking bricks
I was born like the rest
In the neighborhood
To be free and at peace

When a Woman is Fed Up

I have walked long enough
And the road is rough
Still stretching on without end
That sometimes it makes me laugh

Not with joy
But how you play with me like a toy
By failing to fend
For me and our little boy

The imprint of a woman on the floor
Lying near the door
Is me your wife
Sleeping on the floor like a doll

I still walk bare naked
Like no man was ever created
To take care of my life
That I may not be a house that is vacated

I still graze on greens
And your boy gleans
Tins of beef in a rubbish pit
Lest you think he enjoys your beans

I will pack the few I have
And open wide the door to my cave
That whoever desires can come in
And taste the cold waters in my pool of love

A Web of Injustice

Through a window
She saw him enter a hut
Housing a widow
Still hurt
With the death of her love

He held her by the waist
Licking her lips
Down to her breasts
As she breathed with ease
To forget her man gone

She caught him
In broad day light
And like in a dream
Forgave him without a fight
Or grudges against the widow

And through a man next door
He heard of her
Leaning against a pole
Laughing with a man in a car
Whom she had known since childhood

He beat her up
For being faithless
And showed her a map
To her home wearing a dress
Dyed with blood of shame

A Snake in the Forest

Yesterday in this forest
While women gathered wood
They saw a snake coiled in a bird's nest
In no friendly mood

They scared it and angrily
It fled and hid behind branches
Its tongue wagging hungrily
As it waited for chances

Like a nightmare
It swooped and bit a girl above the knee
Leaving its fangs there
Before disappearing into the tree

Blood cascaded down her thighs
And the wound was swelling
Igniting a blast of cries
Because the pain was overwhelming

The Other Woman

She is from the other side of the lake
Light in complexion
And with a lot at stake

What is new I cannot do that she does?
Am I not in full completion
With all the attributes she has?

Although she has broad hips
She cannot win me in a competition
Of sucking a man's lips

She cannot pound sorghum
And maize in a mortar
Or with an axe fell a blue gum

She cannot balance a bucket
Filled with water
Or her neck will break

She cannot till in her own field
Not even half of its quarter
Or her palms will blister and look weird

Let's Talk About Love

Let's talk about love
That snatches joy
From the jaws of pain
That withstands the whirlwind
And flies in the rain

Let's talk about love
That soaks dry lips
With kisses of forgiveness
That embraces the past
And drowns it in forgetfulness

Promise Me My Love

Promise me
You will not love a man again
When I am dead
And buried in the abyss
Without you by my side

Promise me
You will remain
Faithful and take no man to bed
To fondle your buttocks
As I did when alive

Promise me
He will not drink from the well
I dag to widen
Its width when it was narrow
As you parted legs wide

Promise me
You will not smile to any male
Young or old before my ears deafen
And my soul bids farewell
My breath to hide

A Love Poem

You are a piece of paper
On which I want to write a poem
A love poem without ryhme
But that will bring you fame
Never heard of in recent time

I have a fountain pen
That barely runs dry
I will write till ink runs out
In a font that will make you cry
Or for help shout

I will write
Until it vomits ink
And soils you though it were a style
By the time you begin to think
I will have written for a while

I will wait for weeks
To see whether it is prose
Or a poem that was written
Because on a paper anything goes
As long as they fit in

A Man in the House is Worth Two in the Street

A man in the house
Is worth two in the street
They may buy you priceless jewelry
So they can drink from your well
Even when they are not thirsty
Just to feel its depth

They cannot carry you on their backs
When you get sick
Although they may call you hourly
They can never wash your clothes
No matter how dirty
They will only tell you to change

A man in the house
Is worth two in the street
He pays your family cows for dowry
As a vow to be with you all his life
And despite being unwealthy
He shares with you the little he has

He is always by your side in the dark
In the rain or in the pouring heat
Keeping his harvest in the granary
That you may not die of hunger
He strives to keep you healthy
As if fattening you for a purpose

An Encounter with a Mother-in-law

You threw her clothes out
And disappeared in the whirlwind
You broke her silver wares
And vessels to show your clout

You dragged her in the rain
For boys to see her nakedness
And tore off her underwear
To shame the pond we breed children

And when down you kneel
To ask for forgiveness I laugh
When you say you care
And time will heal

The wounds on her skin
I feel insulted as a mother
Because you did swear
You would never again take her in

When you blame it on beer
Birth pangs revisit my womb
And inflict the pain I failed to bear
When I drank a man's sweat for a year

The shame she wore
That rainy day broke my heart
No man can repair
Even if he hit himself against the wall

Lessons worth Learning

A man who marries
A woman with children
Whose father is living
Must not blame her most

When a river is dry
And the rain
Falls in the hills, the water
Passes through the same course

A woman who falls in love
With a man whose former
Wife is pregnant
Must not point a finger at him

When each night he sneaks out
As a diligent farmer
He must water his seedlings
Because his ex is his synonym

The Dream

I saw you in a tree
Seated on a small branch
Like a bird so free
And enjoying the cold breeze
Blowing from the lakeside

I heard your pulse
Echo in my heart
And your face
Shone like lightning
In the cloudless sky

I saw love
In your eyes soaked in tears
And thought like a dove
You would come down
And lean on my shoulder

And display your smile
That I can adore your beauty
For a little while
Or sponge my lips
With your steamy kisses

Before I opened my eyes
To see sunrise peering
Into the window I did realise
It was only a dream
Which just vanished into oblivion

You Lied

You lied when you said
A child is a woman's property
And no man has the liberty
To call him his own

You lied when you said he is her gift
And it is to her he belongs
And no man however strong
May snatch him from her back

You lied when you said
It is only her breast he feeds on
And no matter what a man owns
He cannot nourish him till growth

A child is a man's sweat
His fruit of labor
And no woman however clever
Can call him her own

Nobody's Own

He is your own
A man you own like a vine
When he is in your home

He is nobody's man
When he is sipping wine
He flirts with any woman as he can

It is he who sleeps on your mat
And provides you with needs
When he is in your hut

Make no noise
When he is in the streets
Laughing with women of his choice

On the Wedding Day

Strings of harps
Echo loud in the sky
Contesting with birds perhaps
Or enjoying liberation

Drum beats
Rip bowels open with noise
And like a tremor shake off their seats
In celebration

The bride smiles
To the love of her choice
With whom she has walked miles
Before she could rest on his chest

But there are tears in her eyes
The well is dry
And no driblet at the bottom lies
For her man to quench thirst

Behind a Man's Downfall

Behind a woman's success there's a man
Who buys her costly blouses
That with her shoes match
While he wears torn trousers
There's a man behind a woman's success
Who sleeps dead on a mat of no cost
And lets her sleep alone on a mattress
As it is only she who matters most
There's a woman behind a man's downfall
Who sweeps his house clean
And leaves him as he was before
With nothing but beard on his chin
And returns when he gathers enough wealth
Only to take for all that it is worth

Crying Over Spilt Milk

I saw you at a distance
Flying in the wind like a petal
Disowned at the onset of summer
Looking for a place to settle

I knew that same instance
You walked past the peach tree
Drunk with pride
You would return to plea

You walked out without bye
When you were needed most
And you threw my heart in the trash
Like an item of no cost

And now you kneel down to cry
Over milk that spilt in your pleasure
The love you threw in the garbage
Is another man's treasure

A Virtuous Woman

The beauty in a woman
Is not in the face
Soft like a baby's bottom
And without blemishes

It is in her heart
Where true love lies
Laughing when her man laughs
And crying when he cries

The respect in a woman
Is not in her voice
Voluble and speaking on top of voice
As she bangs doors behind her

It is in her knees
Kneeling when her man calls
And speaking her mind out
Behind closed doors

The strength in a woman
Is not in her brain
Telling her man to do chores
While she knits with friends

It is in her hands
Cooking for her man with passion
And stroking his body
Till he rises to the occasion

The attraction in a woman
Is not her breasts
Or the oval buttocks
Which dance when she walks

It is her acts
She duly performs in bed
And lying on her man's chest
As she sleeps dead

A False Lover

A false lover
Douses thirst with water from your well
And when he becomes a father
He breaks the knot to court another girl

Cover your wells virgins or fall prey
Not all men are worth your trust
They court any woman as they may
Pledging love that long lasts

Only to make her a mattress
They can only use during night time
When bodies without any dress
With darkness rhyme

Who Must Reap the Harvest?

He stood along a path
Proud of his field
That it had given a bumper yield

He dared the dry spell
And cultivated the land
Infested with sand

But she drew his wrath
As she put the matter to rest:
It is not your harvest

Your hoe is stale
And no longer digs deep
I know the man who must reap

He made me miss my bath
Dance a man's dance
And sigh once

I know who made my belly swell
Who sowed his seeds first
And he alone must reap the harvest

Black Pride

You may have a light skin
And wear perfumes
But you can barely cook on kiln
Lest it stains your face with fumes

You may have fine breasts
And broad thighs
But you cannot wear beads
And naked dance before a man's eyes

You may be smart
And look beautiful
But you cannot squat
On his laps when it is needful

You may be wise
And reach greater heights
But you hardly realize
You are incomplete without rites

The Tale of a Chicken

When you want a chicken
Do not buy at the market
It will not roost in your kitchen

Chickens at the market lay eggs
Wherever and whenever
As long as they spread their legs

They have wide groins
And are like trees that grow along the road
Whose fruits nobody owns

When you want a chicken to rear
Buy from the village
It will stay on when you are not there

It will not let other cocks
Roost in its cage
Which is always kept under locks

A Woman's Secret

A boy forgot to take cattle
Out for grazing
His father grabbed a kettle
To douse him with hot water

His mother stood in the way
To take it for him

A girl broke a bucket
On her way to the stream
Her father picked a hatchet
To slice her buttocks

Her mother stood in the way
To take it for her

Because a man cannot prune trees
Without asking his wife
In whose field the seeds
Were sown and grown

The Journey

For Otteria Bwighane Kayuni

She looks at her bare feet
Swollen with wounds of thorns
A pool of tears in her eyes
Overflows and soaks her clothes

She has been walking for long
Passing through deserts and forests
In this winding potholed road
Without a shelter to rest

She walks slowly
Some distance away from her love
Who seems to see glory
At the dead end of the road

The resolute spirit reflected on his face
Offers no hope for her
But he covers every mile by grace
As she trudges in doubt

She looks behind her past
In the times of plenty
When her father's homestead was paradise
To cherish the moments of gaiety

But like Lot's wife
She turns into a pillar of salt
As a shadow of her love riding a chariot
Disappears through the heaven's vault

Fruits of his Labor

She was dry
When in her womb he sowed a seed
He watered it with greed
That it may not die

A seed then, now a tree
With ripe fruits
That look down on the roots
Which made them be

And why should it be incest
To eat fruits of his labor
When his neighbour
Refuses to quench his thirst?

Dust in the Calabash

As she walks in
Her behind dances
To the rhythm of her steps

She scatters her eyes
A wide smile across the edge of the mouth
Glimmers on her red lips

Her bare calabash
Full to the brim with cold beer
Lies on display to the fledglings
Worn out by lust

But ready to quench thirst
Even with a droplet

Each sipping zestfully
She serves the youthful drunkards
Who drink alongside dust

I am not a Child

I am not a child any more
I can throw a spear
A long distance

In the forest of her dreams
She bent to gather fire-wood
While dew was fresh on the grass

Like a mad bull I charged
And from her behind
Threw the spear with strength

She cried in agony
As its sharp head
Pierced through her flesh

She cried even more
When the poison on its head
Soaked in her wound

Blood gushed
And drowned her cries
In a waterfall of laughter

When the Sun Rises

When the sun rises
And birds come out of their nests
To glorify in songs

When dew on the grass summarises
My dream in haste
And away drives it to where it belongs

I will walk in your heart with barefeet
Whose heels cracked and worn out
Leave behind scratches

I will kneel down in defeat
Even when you froth and shout
And fill the grazes with patches

I will not wipe your tears with my tongue
When the pool of love we dug together
Finally dries up in the heat

Everything will stink like dung
As we part even further
And bury our love in a pit

A Foreigner in One's Land

I am a native but a northerner
To you my brethren in the south
Who regard me as a foreigner
Although I am not from without
It is not by design or a wish
To quieten when we meet in town
Or wouldn't I be deemed selfish
If I always walked head down?
Do not lock your sisters in-doors
I will not steal their pride and run away
I can make a good brother in-law
And keep a woman till her hair is grey
Do not think I am not a native
I am your true relative

The Choice of the Heart

She was a rose among thorns
The breasts that jutted from her chest
Once rousing impotent horns
Droop and overlook her waist

She once danced naked at the river
Flying though she had wings
She danced with such vigour
That no man dared touch her bead strings

She refused dowry
From suitors on horse carriage
Who came with cows hourly
To ask her hand in marriage

And let a man within the vicinity
Fondle her breasts
And barter her virginity
For two strings of beads

The Woman Next Door

The more winding the road
The more slippery
And I drag my feet
Through the patches of dry grass

Unaware though
Of who widened it

Footprints of other passers-by
Are visible on the ground
Toes of young boys here
Cracked feet of old men there

The flash floods
That sweep dirt each month
Can barely bury the marks
Deeply engraved

The Train

In the ears cry the bells
Of a train snaking
Through the steel rails

Coughing dark fumes
Through erect nostrils
That cloud over its rooms

And blanket the widows' eyes
Who can hardly see
Where their destiny lies

Along the way
They line up waiting
For their turn to board or stay

In spite of its open windows
Smoke still drifting inside
It fills its belly with more widows

And slowly towing the wagons
Towards the grave-yard
To make the journey a story of bygones

A Word to my Son

Your hand
Is for fondling a woman's breasts
And not punching her with fists

Your chest
Is her pillow when lying in bed
And not a wall on which to smash her head

Your lips
Are for kissing your dear
And not sipping calabashes of beer

Your eyes
Are for admiring the beauty in her face
And not lusting for another woman's dress

You will not eat of this Tree

Of this tree
You will not eat when fruits ripe
No matter how much you care for it

You may look after it
In any way
But someone will reap its fruits

She will come from afar
With an empty basket
And not a hoe to peel its bark

She will pluck the leaves
While you are there
But you will look away in shame

To avoid seeing
The naked branches
You lived washing every season

She will eat of your tree
As long as she lives
Till the roots are dry

A Letcher in the Yard

He followed a woman whose petticoat
He saw hung on a clothes line
And a camisole she had bought
From the street corner

He followed a woman in the forest
Then another in a grape-vine
Gathering fruits in haste
To ask if she was a loner

He followed a woman with a baby
Whose status nothing else could define
And he seemed so ready
To snatch the woman from the owner

How?

A man
Who wears trousers
Without a zipper is ruthless

How
Would he scratch a woman's womb
When it itched?

A man
Who wears a shirt
Without pockets is useless

How
Would he fill a woman's stomach
When it yawned with hunger?

A man
Whose chest is as a snake bare
Without hair is clueless

How
Would a woman rest her head
When she is tired of chores?

She is the Roots

She may be the woman you despise
And spit when she passes by
She may be the woman you often criticize
When she does nothing wrong

She may be the woman you beat
Each night you get home drunk
She may be the woman you deem unfit
To walk with in the streets

She is the roots and believes
In holding you like a tree in spring
And in summer when it sheds leaves
Although she is invisible

A Well by the Roadside

Behind that smile
Are razor-edged teeth
Coated in rust

Her narrow-waisted body
Dark and soft like a baby's cheek
Is a beehive

That keeps not only honey
But a bike of bees
That will sting anything near

She is a well dug by the roadside
That quenches thirst of passers-by
At no cost

Part Two

Messages from no where

Old Sweet Days

Old days are sweet
And need talking about time
And again. Sitting here
Watching a child play in the rain
A dsplay of innocence sparkling on her face

While her elder brothers
Watch over as they sink their lips
In the calabashes of sweet beer
Laughing while she rolls
In the mud in disgrace

The elders sitting around a fire-place
In the middle of the night
Telling tales of a hyena with one ear
While roasting dry maize
And groundnuts to set the pace

The girls born after the sweet days
Scared of the rains hide
In their rooms eaten away by fear
The powder on their faces might wear off
And render their pride useless

In these Times

In these times when a daughter
Fights with her mother
For a man or covers her face
To sleep with her father

When a son pays rent
For his father's mistress
Or takes her out
To rid her heart of stress

When men of God
Declare themselves prophets
And wet dry wombs
Or preach for profits

The elderly's eyes are swollen
And the voice is gone
Weary of laying wreaths
For children who were recently born

The Lazybones

With pride
Chewing emptiness a loafer
Ribs smiling on his chest
Lies under a tree in anger

As hunger
Roosts and lays its eggs
In his granary while his hoe
Lies idle at the corner

She sits by his side
Her collapsing breast
In her baby's mouth
Sucking nothing but air

Their son too is there
Scratching his belly in doubt
If the Whiteman will reopen the door
And loosen his fist

A Funeral of a Mad Man

Wearing sombre faces
And dressed in shame they walk
Carrying a coffin of a beloved one
Who before he could no longer talk
Was next to nothing

He died in the hands of nurses
Who fished him out from a cloud of flies
Playing in his mouth
While others feasted on his eyes
Popping out with starvation

The same women who poked fun
When he dined with mice in rubbish pits
Overwhelmed by grief roll in the dust
Disregarding their outfits
As if it were a contest

They have dressed him a suit
Yet he was left to walk naked in the street
As if he had no siblings of his own
Who hardly lost sleep
When he was missed for months

The Voices

You are toothless dogs
Which call for back up
From their master as they bark

And the tails
Shamelessly hide between the legs
When the frog snores in the hills

Sharpen your teeth
And cut the chains tying your tongues
Spit anger off the chest

And search his pockets
Once empty but now overflowing
With the tenth of the poor's harvest

The fleet of cars
Bought with sweat of the hungry
Who toil day in day out

The Village Spectacle

I yearn for the rain
That smell of earth
When falling afar

The fishermen
Whose pride of wealth
Is in the lake

The village women
Whose faith
Is in the field

And with its harvests
They cheat death
When they silence hunger

I feel for the youth
Whose health
Is eaten away by sins

Digging their own graves
And each making a wreath
No friend will lay

My Mother

My mother
Was raped in the forest
And when she conceived
She choked me with a concoction
Lest she be curst
For parting legs for a stranger

My mother
Cheated on her husband
And when she was deceived
She twisted my neck
And buried me in the sand
To conceal birth

My mother
Whom I loved so much
Was relieved
When she jabbed me with an object
And blood in a gush
Washed away her deed

Fold Your Legs Grandpa

Unless you fold your legs
The youth will not pass
They will stand still
Waiting for their turn to dance

But not until
They realize they are as old
And your legs are still stretched
Refusing to fold

Yet your voice is hoarse
And the grey beard coil
Into your mouth and you cannot walk
Unless your knees are greased with oil

Sundown at Mwenilondo

When it is sunset
At Mwenilondo, a small town
On the edge of the northern county

Lying along the road of fate
That snakes down
Through a mountain

As if to submerge
In the sparkling waters of the lake
Boasting of wealth in her womb

The good image
Whose repute is at stake
Is stained with rust

Women display their wares
By the roadside
Each coercing passers-by effortlessly

As men caught unawares
Take shirts off with pride
In response to the steamy summer

And sip from a single calabash
With women who lost husbands
And part legs for fun

Or douse men's desire for cash

Because their hands
Itch for the currency

They drink with zest
And dance the night long
When noise is wrapped under armpits

Of silence and they curse
As they sing along a song
Awaiting day break

Samples of Fortune

I am coming back from the airport
To see off a trusted friend
Whom I waited for till he left aboard
A chartered plane

He carried with him large sacs
Filled with sample gemstones
To be tested in his lab
To see if they are not bones

It is the third time to come
First he came on foot
Dug the land the size of a dam
And left without leaving a dime

I understood him
He came again to get more samples
And not to pay for the displacement
Of the denizens left in shambles

The second time he came by bike
One dam was flooding
And he refused to build a dike
But got more samples instead

And when he came by plane
I knew he had made a fortune
But he keeps on getting samples
And selling them at the auction

Where is God?

Where is God
When it hurts most?
When His sheep are lost
In the wilderness of deception
And when called
Why doesn't He answer?

When the doors are shut
And the heat
Is burning under my feet
Amidst crying
From the pain in my heart
Why doesn't He hear?

When a girl at the drinking square
Gets rid of a foetus
Slicing it with a pair of scissors
While my womb is barren
And scorched with despair
Why doesn't He see?

When each night
A prostitute like underwears
Changes men and declares
Them hers while I pray for one
And none feels for my plight
Why doesn't He listen?

The Departure

You should have told us
When leaving this place
On your way to the woods
So we could rehearse
The songs the spirits sing

You should have left a word
To the boys or the little girl
You entrusted with your heart
So we could not fail
To explain why you left

The children are asking questions
They didn't hear you yawn
As you always did each morning
You got up to water the lawn
With your garden hose

What should we tell them
When they ask about the jokes
You cracked in the moonless night
About the mysterious fox
That grazed on your maize field?

As we sit around scorning you
For failing to wave goodbye
Burying your footprints
So we cannot know how people die
We remain in the dark

I Will Rest When I am Dead

When I was a girl
With a bare chest
And no bead strings on my waist

I could get up at dawn
While dew was fresh on the lawn
To fetch wood across the border
As my brothers slept dead

I am now a woman
In my prime
And still racing with time

I get up early
And walk in the dark wearily
A hoe on my shoulder
As my husband stays in bed

Kwazulu-Natal Revisited

As I walk along the path
Laden with joy
I have fled the wrath
Of the land owners

Who by virtue of birth
And not skill
Cried songs of death
At the doorsteps of foregners

I cry when over my shoulder
I see a young boy
Cross over the same border
With zeal

Will You Be There?

Will you be there
When hunger bites my stomach
And leaves a scar
That hurts so much
Because nobody seems to care?

Will you be there
When everybody runs away
And keeps their doors ajar
Thinking I am gay
And have no place anywhere?

Will you be there
When my body is weak
And my soul stands at the exit
Trying to sneak
And leave me in despair?

Or you will only be there
When the sun shines on my face
And everybody sees I exist
Filled with grace
And riches to share?

A Living Myth

She awoke amidst a dream
Sucking her thumb
And thinking about nothing

But the stream
Of pee washing away her joy
As she soaks in wet clothing

She cherishes the innocence of youth
And nobody can destroy
The living myth:

A child's evidence
Cannot be denied before the court
Even if she tells lies

Every claim is given credence
Even if she stammers
They will only read from her eyes

Because despite sleeping in a cot
She saw her mother
Wearing another man's coat

In Dilemma

I chased a dancer
Out of my house for a reason
That he always danced for women
Even when it was not a dancing season

I chased a businessman
Out of my house
For sleeping with girls for fun
Coercing them with puffs

I chased a fisherman
Out of my hut
For spending weeks at the lake
While I slept alone on the mat

I chased a farmer
For always coming home tired
And sleeping dressed in summer
Denying my womb the pride of motherhood

I chased a drunkard
For always coming home drunk
Urinating on sheets like a baby
And snoring as though breathing through a trunk

I am now grown up
And living alone without a child
To break my clay cups
And my breasts crave for a man's touch

The Dance

Smoke is coiling
And rising in the atmosphere
And water is boiling
At 200 degrees celcius

It is women brewing beer
Ready for a dance
The dance that is so precious
And no man can dare miss a chance

The dance comes once
In every two harvets
And men are told in advance
To be their guests

The woman with beads in her waist
And the man holding his spear
Dance to their best
As the drum-beats echo in cheer

Waiting with Hope

The dry river may be naked
Without grass in her waist
Or with scattered patches baked
By scotching summer's heat

When dark clouds get together
And blanket the sun in their nest
That no heat pours further
To burn the child's feet

Whose throat dry like a scorched leaf
Yearns for the rains to drop
And bring forth relief
To the game in the bare hills

When whirlwinds blowing roofs away
Calm down and cast hope
To those who had lost the way
And could not trace where stepped their heels

When thunder echoes in the horizon
And lightning tears the sky apart
For nothing but one reason
To bring smiles to the hopeless eyes

The rains shall fall
And fill the river till it is fat
And the grass in her waist shall grow
In praise of the skies

Of Pastors and Offerings

Gathered in a prayer house
A man in his middle age
An air of God's presence in sight
Stands at the pulpit's edge

He came with nothing in his pocket
But his wife by his side
Who keeps his holy books in good custody
And seems to enjoy every word he recites

We came with something in our sacs
Soghum and gourds of sweet beer
Others chickens and priceless linen
As offerings for half a year

We kneel in prayer and in our closed eyes
See heavenly doors open
We give out our gifts and tithes earnestly
And go back home with amen

Do not laugh

Do not laugh
When an old woman displays toothless gums
Or teeth less than enough

She once had a bewitching smile
And teeth for chewing yams
And sugar cane once in a while

Do not laugh
When her beauty fades away with ridges
Or her skin becomes rough

She once had a smooth face
Whose charm men could make pledges
To contest for in a race

Do not laugh
When she walks slowly as if in grief
Or bent on a stick like a dwarf

She once had broad hips
Which left men shake heads in disbelief
And with lust lick their lips

Uhuru Mother, Uhuru

Burning torches graced the night
Then the last cry
Of a cock dying whirred in the lawn
The pain echoed in his heart
As he was left to die
At the break of dawn

Pound grains of millet mother
And put them in the sun to dry
The dark clouds are gone
And the rain is no more
No more lightnings in the sky
Only vultures gleaning the fields of corn

Memoirs of an Immigrant

I am not as free
As a bird in the sky
Which flies up high

I am not as free
As fish in the lake
Which swims for nobody's sake

I am not as free
As a chameleon in the wood
Which crawls as she looks for food

Elegy to the Slave Master

The sun woke up late
And dew on the grass is scarlet

It dripped the night over
And its stale stench still hovers

Lying in a pool of blood is a corpse
Of he who hated us most

He who grabbed our land
And made us plough with hands

Hail the poor coward
Whose blunt sword

Lustful and bored
Sank in his ribs sevenfold

Testimonies

I guided a stranger for a fee
And I was charged with corruption
But this officer let a culprit free
And no one is taking action

I drank a little beer and rode a bike
And I was booked for cycling drunk
But this officer drinks on duty as he likes
And he is not charged because of his rank

I encroached a vine to pick berries
And I was charged with theft
But this officer is embroiled in robberies
And he is just cautioned and scot-free left

On Rwandan Genocide

In a climate of terror
When sons dazed by smoke
Wield uncircumcised tongues
Convulsing in their shorts

Women scatter helter-skelter
Frothing at the mouth with anger
They run into the maize fields
And hide in the dry stalks

A whirlwind of pangs
Swirl at the bottom of their wombs
And in a hasty bite
Chew the joy of motherhood away

The children in whose ears
They sang lullaby to lure them to sleep
Whose toothless gums
They scratched with the tip of their nipples
When they itched with hunger

Whose bottoms
They scrubbed with bare hands
When they irritated with burns
Of their own poo

The cries that pierced the quiet nights
And drummed noise in their ears
While they slept

To draw their attention

Like a snake at the mouth of a nest
Lurk underneath their mothers' petticoats
Ready to tear the wombs
That once housed them

Black Child, Son of Earth

Black child, son of earth
Trust not Samaritans from the west
Who take your ideas in good faith
And modify them to their best
They mine your gems and barter for rifles
To wipe out tribes across the borders
They grab your land by force
And claim to be rightful owners
They stock your clinics with drugs
And subject you to their tests
They exchange your cotton with rugs
As you are regarded the curst
Son of earth, black child
Whom for your complacency do you chide?

At the Crossroads

He sits there
Shaking his head in shame
As he walks down his past

Chest hair
Burnt grey by loneliness
And unquenched lust

He lives in scare
Worried of the winds
Which to his granary brought locusts

That ate all harvests under his care
And the seeds
He had hoped to last

He reclines on his chair
Wishfully thinking
He had kissed the dust

Cries in the Torrents

Alone in the silent hills
Shielded by dry reeds
To hide her deeds
She lies supine

Stars twinkling in the blue
Dazzling her eyes
She chews the barks and cries
As the bitter stench

Strangles a tender neck
Of the unborn
For reasons known
Only to herself

Silence

Silence is golden
When you don't spit dirt
In the ears
Of those you hate

Silence is not forbidden
When you don't roar
In the ears
Of those you know

But silence is a spear
With a sharp end
Which stabs and tears the heart
No sewer can mend

Silence is a thorn
That pierces through the heel
Till it is hurt
And unable to heal

Only My Mother

It was only my mother
Who suffered pangs of birth
As I drew my first breath
To turn a man into a father

She fed me when I was hungry
Washed my clothes when they were dirty
But not until I turned thirty
And her hair became grey

She knew when to laugh
And when I cried she too cried
But when she died
She did not die on my behalf

The Warmonger

He walks bare
As proud as a peacock
Skin and unkempt hair
Black as coke

His camouflage attire
Dirty and old
Displays a desire
To stop the fight for gold

In his eyes
Much as he can recall
He sees smoke rise
And hears cries echo

That ended the wars
Which left many dead
But marked the beginning of woes
That greed bred

The Last Walk

The sublime patches of grey hair
Visible from afar
And wrinkles like ridges spread across my face
Attest I have seen it all:
The seasons of bumper yields
And the whirlwinds that blow off rooftops

They hit their heads against trees
And curse their wombs
Their cries cascading in ripples of tears
Scolding the yawning graves
Which swallow their pride without pity

Their cries echo in the void
As I walk towards the gaping mouth
Leaving behind no footprints
The trees bow and shed leaves
That carpet my path in disgrace

I walk in the shadows of others
Whose souls buried in the wombs
Met the wrath of their mothers' cruelty
The night they swore to spew a man's labor

Dust in the Whirlwind

During the storm, heavy rainfall
We fed on chaff
And drank from dry ponds

Like locusts
Sprayed over with chemicals
Others died in cane fields

Dust wreathed in the whirlwind
And sang in the clouds
As it scattered in all directions

It settled there
Where no one can trace their footsteps
Erased by strong winds

Like Father, Like Son

Made in the image
Of he who toiled in the field
On no wage

He whose sweat
Watered the dry soil
Till it was wet

And sowed his seeds
No other man
Could plant weeds

You only can
Fit in his shoes
And walk in his footsteps as his son

Only if your mother
Did not strip naked in the streets
With little bother

Echoes of a Whisper

A whisper echoed in the night
Calling her by name and damned
She was when over her head set the sun

She had fought a fight
No soldier however armed
Could have won

She stood in death's sight
Without fear of being harmed
Because she knew it was all done

There was no cause for flight
And nothing could have alarmed
A soul that by death had been overran

And in a flashlight
She sprang into the air and away swam
As she bade farewell to her loved one

Printed in the United States
By Bookmasters